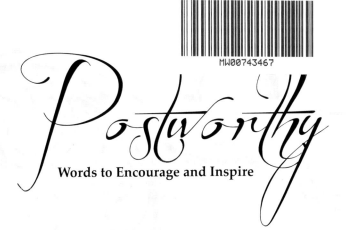

Postworthy

Words to Encourage and Inspire

Wendy K. Walters

Prepared for Publication By

PALM TREE
PUBLICATIONS

Palm Tree Publications is a Division of Palm Tree Productions
WWW.PALMTREEPRODUCTIONS.COM
PO BOX 122 | KELLER, TX | 76244

Unless otherwise noted, Scriptures are taken from the New King James Version (NKJV) of the Bible. Copyright © 1982 by Thomas Nelson, Inc. Used by permission. All rights reserved.

WWW.WENDYKWALTERS.COM

THIS BOOK IS PRESENTED TO

_____

BY

_____

Finally, brethren, whatever things are *true*, whatever things are *noble*, whatever things are *just*, whatever things are *pure*, whatever things are *lovely*, whatever things are of good report, if there is any *virtue* and if there is anything *praiseworthy* — meditate on these things.

—Philippians 4:8

4

You have the power to live every day exercising your gifts and talents as you operate within your passion. Becoming clear about your passion and purpose is a key step. Then you can become intentional with your choices, intentional with your communication, and intentional with the use of your time, talents, energy and resources.

I have been practicing intentional communication for some time. Most mornings I post something inspirational on social media outlets based on my devotions, study and time alone with God. This has become a vehicle to influence others with God's love and encouragement.

Requests to repost, along with the number of comments and private messages I received prompted me to pull some of my posts and compile them into this little booklet for your enjoyment.

I hope that as you read, you too will be motivated and inspired. I invite you to become intentional with your own communication and recognize what a great opportunity you have to touch others with the power of your words.

Wendy

Your *destiny* is not about you. Your personal

mission statement should reflect a purpose greater

than your own fulfillment. To serve at the pleasure of

a King allows that King free access to all your skills,

talents, and resources for the benefit of His kingdom.

To live an *uncommon* life requires

more than talent or mastery of skills.

It requires virtue and an uncommon devotion

to the development of your *character*.

There is no OFF position

on the *genius* switch!

Amazing *grace*, captivating *love*,

overwhelming *peace*...

this is who He is to me!

God let me share a little of this with others

and make their life *brighter* today!

Your *faith* becomes stronger when you share it.

If you want your faith to *grow*,

share what you know!

Preparation time is not wasted time.

Training and *testing*

are part of God's process.

Let patience have its perfect work ... ALL things work

together for good for those who love the Lord and

are called according to His *purpose* !

Morning is a lovely reminder

that God gives us a fresh set of

opportunities each day,

unmarred by mistakes and prepared for new things.

The LORD causes my *thoughts*

to become agreeable

to His will, and so my plans are

established and *succeed.*

(From Proverbs 16:3 AMP)

It isn't so much how much pressure you experience,

but what *effect* that pressure is having on you.

Is it pressing you closer to Jesus? Closer to your destiny?

Toward a change? Thank God for the

pressure and find the flow!

I love sweeping, monumental moves that

advance a process. It is sometimes difficult to be patient

with slow, incremental steps.

I am learning to be *grateful* for each

positive step in the right direction ... after all,

every step moves me closer to the goal.

I have walked by *faith*

and I have walked by sight.

Faith is better!

An encourager *inspires* others with courage,

lifts their spirit, and gives them confidence.

An encourager stimulates others by assistance

or approval. An encourager advances and

promotes the success of someone else.

As you become more *intentional* with your

words and guard what passes the gates of your lips,

do not be surprised if the battle in your mind intensifies.

Bring every thought into captivity to the obedience

of Christ. *Victory* is the reward!

Wisdom hangs out with Prudence,

Knowledge, and Understanding ...

I want these characters to feel welcome in

my home and be my bosom friends!

Fear has disobedience at the root.

If I fear pain, illness, rejection, or lack,

chances are I have not obeyed God's principles that

would protect me in those situations. I fear when

I do not trust God. When I walk in obedience and

love, I do not fear (perfect *love* casts out fear).

I am ready to surrender myself, my influence,

my access, and my abilities to a

purpose greater than myself.

It's going to be a good, good day!

God is in control of *everything* in your life

that is an apparent contradiction.

This is very good news!

Acts of *obedience* on Friday...

fruit/results/reward on Monday. God is SO faithful!

I cannot get enough of Him, His wisdom, and His

presence. His way is *absolutely* the best way!

I may not have the *best* of everything,

but I *make* the best of everything I have!

No matter what the situation, however jumbled or upside

down, the good news is that God's ways will work.

You don't need to try to straighten things out first and

THEN try His plan. You can bring Him your messiest

problem, begin to apply His principles, embrace wisdom,

and see how God will show Himself *strong* to you.

The *secret* to my success can be found

in my constraints, not just in my strengths.

When I recognize these—

submit, surrender, and change,

it moves me closer to my *destiny*!

Do you want more? First ask yourself, "What am I doing with what I have?" God will not *unleash* multiplication until you have demonstrated your ability to steward the increase. (This is not limited to finances.) You must first be found *faithful* with what He has already trusted you to manage before you can possibly be ready for a promotion.

My *anticipation* for what is to

come gives me hope and *courage*!

It is *impossible* for God to lie!

This immutable truth provides hope that is an

anchor for my soul. Like Abraham,

by faith and patience I shall endure to inherit

the *promises* of God!

Beauty Tip:

"Those who look to Him are *radiant,*

their faces are never covered with shame" *(Psalms 34:5).*

Sounds *beautiful* to me!

I *rejoice* even in the valley of the shadow. Why?

If I'm in the shadow, that means I'm in close enough

proximity to the mountain to be *touched* by it's

shadow. I may not be where I want to be, but I can see

where I want to go. Therefore, I rejoice as I set my affection

on things above and move *toward* my goal!

Interruptions are often the devil trying to

interfere with Heaven's *transaction*.

Stay focused and meet your

Divine *appointments*.

Victories are often won in *private*.

It is what is done in the dark places where no one is

watching and you choose the right response. There He

sees and *whispers* your name on the wind.

Anxiety in the *heart* of man causes depression,

but a *good* word makes it glad *(Proverbs 12:25)*.

Spread some good words today ... be a

lifter of someone else's head!

What is a "fold" return? What is meant by

30, 60, or 100 fold? The "fold" consists of

all the *future* fruit that is to come from a thing

(all the offspring, all the harvest, all the return, etc.).

What % of my potential (my fold return to God)

am I *living* up to?

I am *ready* to surrender myself, my influence,

my access, and my abilities to a

purpose *greater* than myself.

Amazing things are in store!

When you stretch, the discomfort of the position makes

you *eager* to return to your normal posture.

When you grow, there's no need to return ...

What you can *now* reach is your *new* normal!

Worry blocks *awareness* of God's presence.

It weighs you down and spoils creative

opportunities.

When compared to the eternal *weight* of

glory, all my troubles (even the substantial ones)

are *light* and momentary. God grant me an

eternal perspective in my day to day journey!

I like to set goals when I am *fresh* and *energized* rather than tired or discouraged. This helps me be *positive* and *proactive*. Then when I am tired or discouraged, I have a set course that guides me so my *mood* doesn't predict my productivity.

41

Can anybody say,

"B - R - E - A - K - T - H - R - O - U - G - H !"

... Don't give up, it is on the way!

I am CONFIDENT of this very thing:

He who began a good work in me

WILL BE FAITHFUL to complete it! That means

I go through, *enduring* the race all the way

until its end ... able to *overcome* and triumph!

Turn down life's *ambient* noise today

and *tune* in to your Creator. You might be

surprised at what He wants to share with you!

God stands *outside* of time. He is not only everywhere at once, He is *"everywhen."* He sees not only your present circumstances, but your past and *future* ones as well. Awesome!

Saying "no" and "not now" are some of the most important things to reaching your *destiny*. Yielding to every request simply because they have merit or are in your power to accomplish can string you out, stress you out, and keep you from *accomplishing* your assignment.

Gratitude creates the *best* atmosphere for

creativity and inspiration. If you're stuck,

pull out all your *blessings* and count

them slowly ... this will spark illumination!

It is really good to know your *secret* weapon. It is even better to know how and when to *wield* it!

Today is a great day to pursue your *passion*

and lift up someone else's countenance. A good

dose of healthy *perspective* can elevate

someone's mood and really make their day!

Moses did not *seek* a dream or his *destiny*, he pursued a relationship with God ... and his destiny *unfolded* before him.

Do what it takes to be *exceptional*.

That means pressing through even when your

energy is gone. Stay *focused* on the goal

... if it's too far away, focus on a closer goal that

takes you in the *direction* of the bigger

goal. Keep moving forward, don't give up!

God's promise to me today:

"... I will *strengthen* you. Yes, I will help you.

I will uphold you with my righteous *right* hand."

(Isaiah. 41:10)

Every time God promotes us or increases our measure of *influence*, it is because He has people in mind ... people you are *equipped* to touch with His love and grace. God loves people!

Investing in the *success* of another person

fills you with energy and joy.

Touching another person with what you have inside

is the surest way to *receive* new insight.

I am *keenly* aware of the Source

of every good and perfect thing in my life ...

and I am *totally* grateful!

A small change today could bring about a

dramatically different tomorrow!

Life is a process. Building things that last takes time.

Don't give up when results are not *instant*

...you WILL reap in due season if you faint not.

The results of a day lived well compound as surely

as interest on money *invested* well.

The best of all possible uses for a *home* is to *fill* it to the brim with family and friends that make it overflow with *love* and *laughter*.

I am often called a *dreamer*, and that is usually meant as a compliment. However, since I pursue dreams until they become a *reality*, my conclusion is that the only *true* realists are dreamers!

Rest is an important key to success.

The hamster in the wheel only THINKS he's gettin'

somewhere with all that energy!

Rest, plan, then work hard with *focus*.

When your subconscious is

argumentative and trying to

convince you of something, it isn't God's voice.

His voice is self-authenticating and fills you with

peace. While this may not help you hear God,

it WILL help you discern what is NOT God.

Responding to God's *whispers* always results in the favor that only comes with obedience. Turn down the noise around you, *listen* for His voice, and follow.

I find my *motivation* internally.

I would do what I do even if it wasn't my job.

I *push* myself harder than any coach ever

could. This is why I will *succeed*!

Have you ever noticed that the difference

between *excitement* over a dream

and *frustration* is in the ability to

fund the dream? Resourcefulness is a key to your

success. It's the entrepreneur's hallmark.

If someone is too *tired* to give you a smile,

leave one of your own, because no one

needs a *smile* as much as

those who have none to give.

When you are behind enemy lines and you

approach the border and *freedom,*,

your enemy *strengthens* his attack:

dogs, snipers, razor wire, mines ... all to discourage

your *pursuit* of freedom. Keep running!

Few things *diminish* dreams like the daily grind of life's responsibilities. Of course, maintain your responsibilities, but take out that *dream* every single day and *remind* yourself of why it is your dream. Each day, no matter how small the increment, move *toward* that dream.

Today may I find *opportunities* in the events of everyday life,

and having seen them, may I seize them.

It is *impossible* to go the extra

mile if you haven't gone the first.

Remember Abraham:

God *always* comes through, always fulfills His

promise ... even when it may seem to take longer

than we're comfortable with. Take heart.

Endure.

We must *expect* the power of God

if we are going to *connect*

with the power of God!

Pardon is a *powerful* thing.

To walk then above the reproach of

your guilty past is the most *grateful,*

honoring response possible.

Progress is sometimes by great *leaps* and *bounds* and it feels so good!

Sometimes it comes inch by steadfast inch. Staying *committed* to the process, working hard, and

keeping your eye on the prize is a sure recipe for a win.

Scars are not just evidence of *pain*,

they are evidence that you've been *healed*.

"A morning-glory at my window satisfies

me more than the metaphysics of books" *(Walt Whitman).*

To *experience* a thing is far better than a

mere study. Know God. Experience Him today!

Listen and obey. Such simplicity.

Such *joy* to know that One who knows all things

carries my *destiny* in His hand.

I have but to get out of the way and cooperate

with His *perfect* plan.

Opportunity is often *disguised* in

every day garments and looks suspiciously like work!

Anxiety indicates *dwelling* on something

where God is not present or powerful.

No matter your circumstance or situation,

trust God in the moment and allow

that beautiful *peace* that surpasses

understanding to guard your heart and mind!

Guess what happens when a procrastinator

gets a really good idea? ...*nothing*!

Engage *actively* and presently.

Partner with an activator, find an encourager

... but by all means *engage*!

Today you have the opportunity

to make a *positive*

difference in somebody's life.

Will you seize it?

Opportunity meets preparation.

I say this often because it's true.

Live intentionally.

Live on *purpose*!

Is your life shattered? Nothing but broken pieces?

God will create a beautiful *mosaic* from

all those broken pieces. It will be a

one-of-a-kind, breathtaking, awe-inspiring masterpiece.

Take *heart* friend, you're the mosaic!

Your *destiny* is like a piece of a jigsaw puzzle. Your piece fits into the larger picture of something greater than yourself. This does not diminish the beauty and uniqueness of your piece, but until you *yield* to being "locked in" to other pieces, you cannot experience the joy of the wholeness you were created for.

Embrace the *possibility* of failure as a gem in the process. Failure is often a success that just hasn't grown up yet. Put your *efforts* into things that are worthwhile. Risk failure. It's worth the outcome!

Enthusiasm is present in creation.

Atoms, the building blocks of all matter, have protons,

neutrons, and electrons dashing about in a

choreographed dance! The earth *sings*

together in heaven's rhythm!

A baby step for you may be a giant *leap*

for someone else. Whenever possible,

encourage others to take the next step,

without judging the degree of difficulty or

measure of *faith* required based on

your own life story. Forward is good!

Knowing *God* and His greatness is the most

fulfilling thing I know. Understanding that He has

accepted me and adopted me into His family leaves

me completely *secure* and filled with joy!

"I would go to the deeps a hundred times to *cheer* a downcast spirit. It is good for me to have been afflicted, that I might know how to speak a word in *season* to one who is weary."

~C.H. Spurgeon

We live in a world where a *word* from God changes reality. A world that *adjusts* effortlessly to His thoughts and intentions. Could I be like the centurion, "... only say the word and my servant will be healed"? May I grasp the *magnitude* of what this means!

Dealing with problems, crises, and conflicts

builds *strength* in you and causes you

to advance. This is the process of success.

You have *significance*.

It is often hard to see how what we do

(particularly in the small things) makes a difference.

But our *obedience* to God's call in

combination with everyone else's faith-filled

response is all part of His purposeful plan.

Too many people I meet are *waiting*

for opportunities instead of

working toward them.

A fish is a *genius* in the water, and a total failure in the grass. Discover and focus on the genius in your children ... each one of them is *wired* for genius in some capacity and they'll never know it unless someone points it out and *celebrates* it.

The best way out is t-h-r-o-u-g-h!

Every step in the *right* direction

(no matter how small) brings you

closer to your goal. Take heart!

Your greatest *influence* occurs when you

mix obedience to God with great humility. When

you are keenly aware of the *grace* of God on

your life and His destiny is activated inside you,

you will change *atmospheres* and leave

the imprint of Christ on all you encounter.

I have found that being skeptical keeps people safely

grouchy and steeled against the possibility of the

miraculous in their lives. In erecting walls to

avoid being "duped" by things supernatural, they also

avoid being blessed. I choose to remain *open* to God's

power and I look for the miraculous in every day life.

Even when my thoughts are totally occupied with the *business* at hand ... God's thoughts are still on me. While I am captured by the affairs of life, God is *thinking* of me. Wow!

Your self-talk guides your choices. You must

program your mind with resourcefulness,

favor, creativity, and opportunity. This "re-wires"

you to be *aligned* with heaven's destiny.

Life has a *rhythm*. Periods of work and rest.

Periods of growth and dormancy. Productivity

and wheel spinning. Success and failure. This is

good. This is God's plan. Whatever *season*

you are in, know that it is part of the plan, part

of the rhythm and necessary for wholeness.

When opportunity arrives, the time for preparation

is past. Prepare *now*. Prepare for your dreams

before the opportunity presents itself.

That way, when called on to perform,

you are *ready* in season.

Adversity has a way of bringing *forth* talents

and ingenuity that would remain dormant

if prosperous circumstances always

prevailed. Adversity is a *gift*.

Forget about what's *easy* and don't be bogged down

by what seems impossible. Focus instead on what is

do-able, even though *difficult*.

Do the things that are worth doing

and success will follow.

Wendy is an author, speaker, and entrepreneur. Her destiny lies in helping others identify their passion and discover their gifts. With this information, she factors in developed skill sets and helps people articulate their dreams. Her unique gift translates dreams into tangible reality and point others confidently toward their destiny. She finds no greater joy than seeing others released into their purpose and living 100% fully alive!

Wendy

TO LEARN MORE:

WWW.WENDYKWALTERS.COM